NAME

NAME   *guesses*   THOUGHTS

Guesses

Glasses

NAME   *guesses*   THOUGHTS

NAME

Guests

THOUGHTS

guesses

THOUGHTS

NAME   *Guesses*   THOUGHTS

NAME	*Guesses*	THOUGHTS

NAME

Guesses

THOUGHTS

NAME   Guests   THOUGHTS

NAME   guests   THOUGHTS

NAME   *guesses*   THOUGHTS

NAME   *Guesses*   THOUGHTS

NAME   *guesses*   THOUGHTS

NAME

Guesses

THOUGHTS

NAME   *Guesses*   THOUGHTS

NAME   Guesses   THOUGHTS

NAME   *Guesses*   THOUGHTS

NAME   *Guesses*   THOUGHTS

NAME   *Guesses*   THOUGHTS

NAME

Guesses

THOUGHTS

guests

NAME   *Guests*   THOUGHTS

NAME   *Guests*   THOUGHTS

Guests

NAME   *Guests*   THOUGHTS

Guesses

Guests

Guesses

NAME   Guesses   THOUGHTS

NAME   *Guesses*   THOUGHTS

NAME

THOUGHTS

NAME   *Guests*   THOUGHTS

NAME   *Guesses*   THOUGHTS

Guests

NAME   *Guesses*   THOUGHTS

Guests

NAME   Glasses   THOUGHTS

NAME   *Guests*   THOUGHTS

NAME | Guesses | THOUGHTS

Guesses

NAME   *Guesses*   THOUGHTS

Guests

NAME   *Guesses*   THOUGHTS

Guests

NAME   *guesses*   THOUGHTS

NAME   *guesses*   THOUGHTS

NAME   THOUGHTS

NAME   *guesses*   THOUGHTS

NAME   *Guesses*   THOUGHTS

Made in the USA
Monee, IL
19 December 2019

19146575R00057